OUT
ENC

MW00915524

FIBER OPTIC
COMMUNICATIONS
HISTORY, THEORY, AND APPLICATION

RE LEWIS

OUTSIDE PLANT ENGINEERING 101

CONTENTS

OUTSIDE PLANT ENGINEERING 101

OUTSIDE PLANT
ENGINEERING

INTRODUCTION

The intent of this guide on the history, theory, and application of fiber optic cable is to introduce the new Outside Plant Engineer to the importance of fiber optic cable in Outside Plant Engineering and the Telecommunications industry.

In future additions to the Outside Plant Engineering 101 series, more detailed elements and responsibilities will be covered in order to expose the OSPE to the duties and requirements of their job an Outside Plant Engineer.

Books currently in progress, or already published in this series, are:

Outside Plant Engineer Job Descriptions

Conventional Cable Transmission for the OSPE I

Taking Field Notes for the OSPE I

Aerial Plant and Guying for the OSPE II

FTTX Planning and Design for the OSPE II

Project Management for the OSPE III

OUTSIDE PLANT ENGINEERING 101

Author RE Lewis spent over 40 years in the Communications industry as an Outside Plant Engineer or Engineering Manager.

Lewis was a contract OSPE in the 70's, a Sprint Project Engineer in the 80's, an AT &T Manager, Engineering and Planning in the 90's and 2000's, and a Network Instructor for AT&T University in the 2010's. With US Sprint, Lewis was a Project Engineer on the team that designed and built the United States' first coast to coast fiber optic communications network. Lewis served as an OSPE, a project Manager, Network Instructor, or Special Projects Program Manager until retirement in 2022.

History of Fiber Optics

1880's

The Photophone was an innovation that Alexander Graham Bell Patented in 1880. The system made use of mirrors that vibrated due to the pressure of the sound waves from the speakers. A photocell in a phone receiver received a vibrating light signal from mirrors that were transported via the atmosphere. A speaker was powered by an electric current that was linked to this.

Unfortunately, it turned out to be both too unreliable and impractical to transport light through the atmosphere.

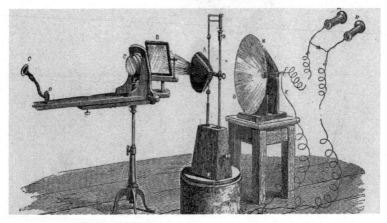

1920's

The concept of transmitting pictures for television
facsimile transmission

utilizing arrays of hollow pipes or transparent rods
was patented by

John Baird and Clarence Hansel in the 1920s.

1930's

In Germany in the 1930s, the first optical fiber picture transmission was recorded. It was a picture of a lightbulb. The project was abandoned because of the poor picture quality and transmission from the fibers.

The use of transparent cladding over the glass or plastic fiber was established as a result of later optical fiber transmission experiments. With a transmission attenuation of just 1 decibel per meter, this significantly enhanced transmission.

The 1950's and 60's

In the 1960s, television sparked an enormous demand for the transmission of more information at a quicker rate. The expanding telephone network turned to a higher frequency to carry more traffic and the needed additional capacity.

There was extensive usage of microwave and radio frequencies at the time. Once the laser was created in 1958, it appeared that the 1960s would witness a tremendous advancement in fiber optic technology.

Unfortunately, fiber optics technology was shown to have too much loss of signal for telecommunications. In 1964, Cr. Charles Cowl proposed the hypothesis that the imperfections inside the glass strands, rather than the glass itself, were what produced the loss of signal in fiber optics.

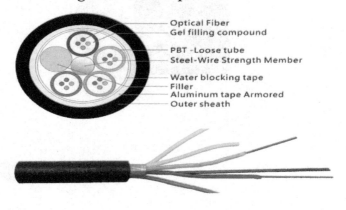

1070's

Using the idea behind Dr. Cowl's research, Corning Glassworks said in 1970 that they had created single-mode fibers with a significantly lower loss. A method of drawing glass strands that produced significantly fewer glass imperfections was invented by them. This made it possible for researchers, engineers, and innovators to create a fiber optic system that started to satisfy the needs of the telecommunications sector.

The initial optical telephone communication system was set up in 1977. The project transported data 1.5 miles beneath Chicago's downtown. A voice channel equivalent of 672 was carried by each optical fiber.

1980's

Three years later, in 1981, that speed was raised to 140 Mbps.

America's telecom providers started putting in a network that could run at 400 Mbps in 1983.

By 1985, 400 Mbps was the standard rate for long-distance transmission.

In 1986, AT&T sent 1.7 billion bits per second on fibers that were designed to deliver 400 Mbps.

1990's

Bell Labs claimed transmitting 10 billion bits per second in 1993.

Bell Labs, NTT Labs, and Fujitsu reported transferring 1 trillion bits per second in 1996.

2 terabits were sent in 1998, while 3.28 terabits were transmitted in 2000.

The 2000's

Every two years, technology doubles the speed of data transmission. If things continue as they are, data transmission rates will reach over 600 terabits per second by the year 2024. At such speed, it would be possible to transmit all of humankind's written works multiple times in a single second.

Major carriers' advancing technologies in use today are always calling for faster speeds and greater capacity. Fiber optic networks, including Fiber To The Premise, Fiber To The Cell, Fiber To The Business, and Fiber To The Node, are crucial to upcoming high capacity services.

Beyond 2022

The enhanced data transmission speed is only the beginning.

Laser technology and fiber fabrication are two areas where technology has

advanced significantly. Passive Optical Networks with Gigabit capabilities will be the norm in all telecom markets and with all carriers.

To keep up with the most recent technological advancements, electronic switches cannot work swiftly enough. A need for fresh developments in switching technology results from this.

This implies that for our business to remain competitive, more and more fiber must be installed.

MODERN FIBER TECHNOLOGY

Three key technologies have led to the development of modern fiber technology.

1. The development and improvement of the laser

2. Integrated circuits that allow electronic devices to be smaller because of their use

3. Creation of superior fiber optic cable

The main elements of today's fiber optic networks in the telecommunications sector are these technologies. This network transforms electrical information signals into light signals using a light source that travels via glass fibers inside the network.

Transmission of voice and data requires a durable, high-capacity transmission channel. Through extended distances, conventional transmission over copper wires may experience significant signal loss.

COPPER vs. FIBER

Copper	Fiber
Copper installation is more difficult	Allows more signals to be transmitted free of errors
High loss of signal over long Distances	Fiber provides a higher level of Security
Can be an electrical Hazard	Not a conductor of electricity
	Fiber is smaller and lighter
	Eliminates loss and distortion

Copper Cable

24 circuits are carried on two cable pairs in digital transmission

systems like copper T1 carrier/DS1.

To maintain an exact signal level using copper wire, repeaters are needed around every mile along the transmission line. Regenerators need to be swapped out as transmission speeds vary.

Fiber Optic Cable

Fiber strands are not a conductor - glass is an insulator. Fiber eliminates the electrical danger since it does not conduct electricity. In addition to safety, Installation is made simpler by fiber's smaller and lightweight size. One of the greatest advantages of optical fiber is that loss and distortion are almost eliminated.

FUTURE GROWTH

Certain benefits are crucial for the fiber optics industry's future expansion.

These include a lower bit error rate (BER), which enables the error-free transmission of more signals. A nearly infinite bandwidth capacity is available.

Additionally, fiber is immune to interference and may travel farther without repeaters. Optical fibers also offer the highest level of security.

As more fiber is laid and the cost of maintenance decreases, fiber is becoming more and more cost-effective. New cables can be deployed considerably faster and more effectively because of their lightweight and compact dimensions.

Finally, it is simple to upgrade the bandwidth as more bandwidth becomes available.

Principals of Digital Transmission

The use of fiber technology has significantly improved telecommunications operations. This chapter will help you grasp digital technology in order to completely comprehend fiber optics.

Fiber optics are driven by digital technologies.

The optical light is turned on and off by the digital input signal. Despite the differences in nomenclature between digital technology and fiber optics, it is crucial to understand the fundamentals of digital technology.

Sending signals between two devices to exchange information is known as communication. Analog and digital signals are two that you might be familiar with. Because it can be retrieved, rectified, and amplified more readily and is more noise-resistant than an analog signal, a digital signal is superior to an analog signal. Because of this, currently, the trend is to convert an analog signal to electronic data.

Three fundamental components are required for the transmission system to deliver and receive signals:

Transmitter: A device that transforms information into signals before transmitting those signals,

Receiver: A device that receives the signal being broadcast and converts it back into the data being delivered,

Transmission Path: The Link, or facility, that connects the transmitter and receiver.

A digital signal is used to send information from the transmitter to the receiver.

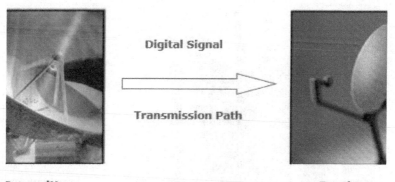

Digital Signal

Transmission Path

Transmitter   Receiver

SIGNAL REGENERATION

Digital signals are impacted by distortion, noise, and loss.

A regenerator or regenerative repeater can be used with a digital transmission to produce a new signal from a sample of the old signal.

Digital technology sends a clearer representation of the voice stream, which reduces loss, noise, and distortion.

Positive and negative pulse-based digital regenerative repeaters reproduce the signal based on a sampling, while excluding noise and distortion.

Because the regenerator has a predetermined threshold for the input signal, loss, noise, and distortion are removed. The input signal must surpass the chosen threshold for a certain period.

FIBER STRAND MAKEUP

Super-pure glass strands known as optical fibers offer a low-loss channel for the transmission of optical signals. An optical fiber's Core, Cladding, and protective Coating make up its usual cross-section.

The Core: The Core is composed of geranium-doped silica, and serves as the path for the optical signal. The core is encased with cladding.

The Cladding: Cladding is likewise formed of silica glass but has somewhat different optical transmission properties. The optical signals are primarily kept inside the core by the boundary between the glass core and glass cladding and their distinct optical transmission properties.

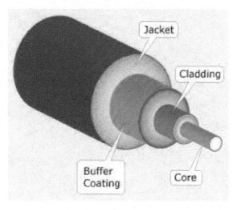

The Coating: The exterior of the cladding is covered with a polyurethane finish. It guards against fiber damage during handling, wiring, and installation. Following installation, the coating shields the fiber from the environment to maintain its structural and optical qualities.

Depending on the manufacturer's standards, the coating's width is typically 226 microns or more in diameter. The diameter of a human hair is about 100 microns, which is about the same width as the core and cladding of a fiber.

FIBER PLACEMENT

Aerial, Direct Buried, Conduit, and Submarine are the four main settings in which fiber placement in OSP takes place. Local policy, preferences, budgets, and existing plant can be factors in the choice of placing. Typically, however, the geographic environment will determine the placement method of new outside plant.

Each of these settings has distinct qualities and necessitates a separate set of deployment techniques.

OUTSIDE PLANT
ENGINEERING

Placement Environment

Aerial: Utility poles and the supporting strand are used to suspend cables above the ground. The cable is tied to a metallic strand that is fastened to the poles. It is possible to order the strand already fastened to the cable. Self-supporting cable is what it is termed.

Buried: With little to no physical protection, the cable is direct buried into the ground. It is buried at a depth of at least 24" for distribution fiber (F2), and a depth of 36" for cable carrying trunk, interoffice and special design circuits (F1).

~ 29 ~

Underground: The conduit is filled with cable (a protective pipe system usually encased in concrete). Conduit can be 36" or deeper below the surface, and manholes can be used to access it periodically so that the cable can be inserted and joined and maintained.

Submarine: In an aquatic setting, such as a lake or ocean, the cable is laid on the lake or ocean floor. The outer sheath is made to withstand the rigors of being submerged in water.

FIBER CABLE BENDING RADIUS LIMITATIONS

Ensuring the bend radius is not exceeded when putting fiber is crucial. Excessive attenuation or breaking may result from this. The bend radius must meet two conditions, one of which is static and the other of which is dynamic.

Dynamic: Utilized while installing cables, the bend radius must be at least 20 times the cable's outer diameter.

Static: Utilized when the cable is already placed, and the radius must be at least ten times the cable's outer diameter.

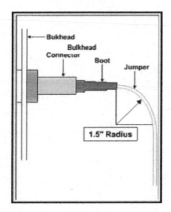

FIBER CABLE PLACEMENT
CATEGORIES

Local Loop (also known as Exchange Cable in your area) and **Interoffice Cable** make up the majority of the fiber that construction and engineering divisions install.

Similar to copper, a local loop is a fiber that is installed outside of the wire center's borders from a central office. A building, a Controlled Environmental Vault (CEV), an outside plant cabinet, or another structure inside the wire center can be used to terminate the fiber.

Interoffice Fiber (IOF) is fiber installed from one central office to another central office across the wire center office borders. The owner of the other central office may be AT&T or one of several independent businesses, such as Verizon or Windstream.

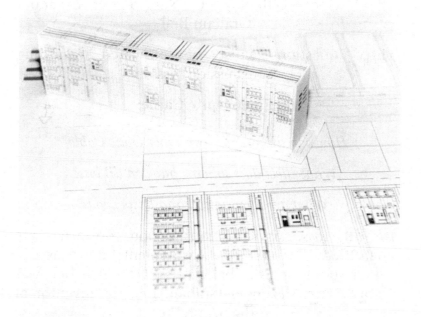

Transmission Impediments

dB Loss

dB = Decibel = 1/10 of a bel – Named after Alexander Graham Bell

Three questions must be answered regarding transmission loss on

Fiber Optic Cable:

How can dB loss occur in Fiber Optic Cable?

What effect does splicing have on dB loss?

What are Attenuation and Dispersion?

In dB loss, optical transmission obstacles are quantified. The unit of measurement known as dB, which stands for decibel and is 1/10 of a bel, was named after Alexander Graham Bell the inventor of the telephone.

A gain is represented by a positive number of dBs, whereas a loss is represented by a negative number of dBs.

The measuring unit of a decibel is the ratio of two voltages, currents, or powers.

TRANSMISSION IMPEDIMENTS

Data is sent by a light beam in optical technology. To represent the binary ones and zeros, the beam is either on or off. A pulse stream is made up of

several binary codes.

An imaginary line representing the direction of moving light is defined by a

Laser light ray.

For instance, a ray indicates the path of the sun's light beam as it passes through trees or buildings.

Imagine a little, bright region of the ground that is surrounded by shadows, with the sun's rays passing through the tree branches to illuminate it. Only a small portion of the tree's limbs and leaves allow light to enter.

The fiber cladding and coating similarly guide the pulse stream of light to move into the glass core.

DISPERSION

Light tends to disperse as it leaves the medium from which it came.

The term for this is dispersion.

The majority of light disperses as it goes farther. The density of a light ray remains conical. This is what occurs when you watch a movie. To display on a bigger scale, the light disperses after passing through the film.

The beams of light travel at the same speed or velocity in a vacuum and free space, respectively. The speed or velocity is lower in physical substances like glass or water than it is in space.

While all wavelengths of light move through space at the same speed, various wavelengths of light move through materials at varying speeds. Refraction and reflection are the results of this speed reduction.

REFRACTION

Refraction is an optical illusion that makes what you see appear to be bent. When light transitions from one medium to another, something happens.

Refraction occurs when a light beam crosses a border between two media when the velocities of the two media are noticeably different.

A prism is created by one media. It causes a dB loss at the distant end by deflecting the light ray.

A water straw is a nice illustration. The straw looks to bend or change direction when it contacts the water.

REFLECTION

Reflection is light that is bent back or bounced off will reflect. It happens where low speed and fast speed meet.   A picture in a mirror is one illustration.

Another illustration is peering through a window. Fresnel reflection is the name given to this kind of reflection.

According to Fresnel theory, glass allows 90 percent of light to travel through while only allowing 3 percent to bounce back. When peering through a window made of glass, on the glass, there is a faint reflection that can be observed.

SPLICING

Reflection and/or refraction may occur as a result of a poor mechanical or fusion fiber splicing or mechanical connections.

An optical time domain reflectometer (OTDR) can be used to identify a faulty splice.

Reflection will appear as a spike on the OTDR. The dB loss increases as the

surge heightens.

A reflective loss of -40dB or better is considered acceptable. The better, the greater the negative number.

OUTSIDE PLANT ENGINEERING 101

Fiber splice integrity and loss is measured by an Optical Time Domain Reflectometer (OTDR) and a report is produced to document the transmission characteristics of the circuit.

Splices - The Greatest Contributors of dB Loss

Splicing may account for a significant portion of the overall dB loss. dB loss is less   of an issue with more recent fusion splicing and mechanical connectors.

When fibers are spliced together, irregularities that might occur throughout the   manufacturing process can result in dB loss.

For instance, there would be a considerable loss at the connecting site if two fibers were made with differing diameters and then spliced together.

Additionally, if the fibers are out of line and split at the splice,

there might be a large loss.

It is essential to plan carefully to reduce loss. They should be devoid of

defects or roughness brought on by fiber cutting.

MACROBENDS AND MICROBENDS

Macrobends: The fiber cable can have massive bends called macro bends. Light exits into the cladding if the curve exceeds the bend radius or is too tight for the fiber cable. Construction must avoid bending fiber cable to a radius that is less than 10 times the outside diameter of the fiber cable in order to avoid damage.

A 0.5" diameter wire, for instance, shouldn't deviate from a 5"

minimum bend radius.

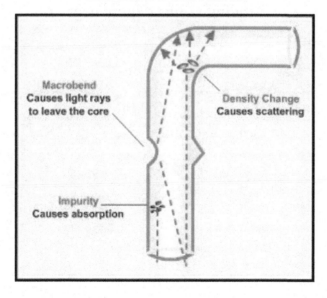

Macrobends may result from the stretching of the fiber over minute lumps or flaws in the cable material during the cabling procedure.

The majority of flaws are made during the manufacturing process.

Macrobends, however, might result by adding kinks or flaws while stretching wire during installation.

Microbends: are smaller bends that damage fibers and are typically introduced during the placement process by physical impact or violating established minimum bending radius requirements.

POLARIZATION

Light waves vibrate and spread forth in all directions from the sun or light. Light is considered to be polarized when vibrations are aligned into one or more planes of direction, regardless of how it is transmitted, dispersed, refracted, or reflected.

Polarization of light can occur naturally or intentionally. An instance of natural polarization may be seen when observing a lake. The light that escapes the water's filter is reflected in the glare off the surface. Although the water may be clear, you may frequently not see below the surface for this reason.

A polarizing filter only lets through the light that matches its orientation, as seen in the picture above, as an example of polarization. Only the portion of the light wave that is aligned with the filter's slots is let through. The light that was transmitted is regarded as polarized. Light waves that vibrate only in one plane are known as polarized waves. The waves that makeup plane polarized light all have the same direction of vibration.

MODAL DISPERSION

Modal Dispersion comes from light going farther in one certain mode of fiber than another, and it gets bigger as the fiber gets longer. The output pulse is broader than the input pulse when measured there. Dispersion restricts the bandwidth of the fiber since the pulse stream will ultimately spread to the point that the individual pulses are no longer recognizable from one another. Consider this to be a route, where light can go on a variety of paths, some of which will take longer to reach their destination than others.

Reduceing the diameter of the core until the fiber can propagate one mode effectively is one method of reducing modal dispersion. The diameter of a single mode fiber core is around 2 to 8 nanometers. It varies in direct proportion to how quickly information is transferred.

For instance, the usual bandwidth of an 850/1300 nm multimode system is 400 MHz. A single mode 1310/1550 nm system could offer limitless bandwidth.

This disparity in bandwidth is brought on by modal dispersion.

Waveguide Dispersion

Waveguide Dispersion occurs when light waves moving through the core-cladding boundary or in the cladding arrive at the receiver at various times, dispersion has taken place. This was a typical issue with LEDs, but since lasers were invented, this kind of dispersion has been diminished.

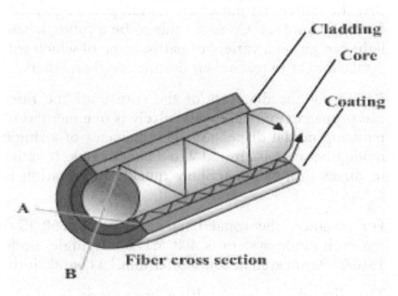

CHROMATIC DELAY DISPERSION

It refers to describing the hues or wavelengths of an optical source.

The spectrum of colors has a variety of wavelengths.

Light beams of various wavelengths go along fiber at various rates, as seen in the diagram. The light pulse widens out more as it travels throughout the length of the cable the wider the wavelength range submitted.

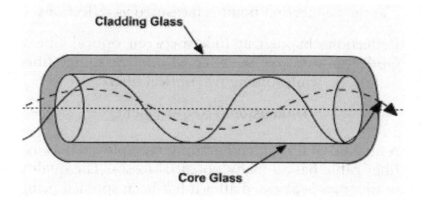

Cladding Glass

Core Glass

REFLECTIONS

The Greek mathematician Euclid, who carried out several experiments about 300 BC, is credited with some of the first descriptions of light reflection. Euclid appears to have had a thorough grasp of how light is reflected. But it wasn't until 1,600 years later that the Arab scholar Alhazen put forward a rule outlining precisely what occurs to a light beam when it meets a flat surface and then bounces off into space: A fraction of incident light that is reflected into the source fiber at the connection point is measured as reflections.

Reflections happen at links between optical fibers. Optical power may be reflected into the source fiber while joining two optical fibers.

Dimensional Requirements

A method of testing and grading is employed because fiber cable has so many potential losses. The quality of the fiber is assessed after it has been spooled using measurements and grading.

The most crucial test is the one for the dimensional requirements since discrepancies might lead to a variety of issues.

The ovality scale determines how far the cross-section of the fiber core or cladding is from being perfectly spherical.

How effectively the core is centered inside the core cladding is determined by concentration.

Other Tests

To establish if there are or will be transmission barriers, further tests are performed, such as:

Tensile strength (Fiber strength)

Bandwidth quantifies the fiber's capacity to transport information.

Chromatic dispersion is the distribution of different light wavelengths

across the core.

The Refractive Index profile calculates numerical accuracy and

checks for optical flaws.

Attenuation or dependency on temperature size of the cable.

EQUIPMENT

There are certain sorts of tools required for transmission and connection while working with fiber optics. Connectors, jumpers, and connectivity tools are some of them (including distribution frames and optical termination panels).

Let's begin by looking at connectors:

To connect fiber jumpers to the connected equipment, connectors from four main groups are employed. Threaded, Bayonet, Push-Pull, and Duplex are among them.

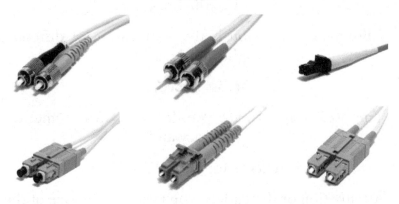

There are several connection styles within each category:

The threshold includes FC, D4, SMA, and Bionic.

Bayonet style includes ST connectors

Push-Pull includes SC, and

Duplex includes FDDI, SC Duplex, and ESCON

In addition, there are LC and MPO (Multi-fiber Push On) connectors.

LC connectors are used on Next Generation SONET equipment, OPT-E-MAN™, and ATMs.

MPO connectors contain multiple fibers in a single connector and are used in specialized configurations.

INDUSTRY STANDARDS

As is with most fiber optic equipment, major carriers have standard optical connectors that are used.

Category	Style
Threaded	FC, D4, SMA, Biconic
Bayonet	ST
Push-Pull	SC
Duplex	FDDI, SC Duplex, ESCON

Lightwave transmission systems employ SC connectors to connect, detach, and reattach fiber optic cables with the least amount of loss.

Two optical fibers are physically aligned to light one another to create an optical connection.

You may buy connectors in pigtail or jumper cable form. Pigtails allow you to create your cable with two different types of connections at either end if desired. Pigtails feature a connector at one end and bare fiber at the other.

Loss Associated with Connectors

Loss in a fiber connection to be determined by several factors:

Separation Loss may result from optical fiber separation. A little contact between fibers results in the best coupling.

Lateral Alignment is the misalignment of optical fibers. This is one of the greatest contributors to connector loss.

Angular Alignment optical loss is minimal in biconic connectors. Nominal angular misalignment is less than .2 degrees.

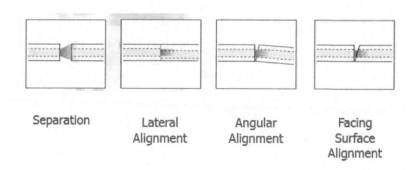

Separation Lateral Angular Facing
     Alignment Alignment Surface
                Alignment

Facing Surface Alignment is when there are scratches on the facing surfaces or there is contamination of these surfaces by dust, fingerprints, oil, or other matter. This can cause excessive loss.

MAINTAINING INTEGRITY

The following are a few crucial actions to insure system integrity:

Maintain the appropriately aligned, pristine, and unharmed polished optical surfaces.

Never touch a connector's smooth optical surface.

The optical fiber cannot rotate while the SC and ST connections are being joined thanks to a mechanical key.

Store protective coverings at the scene in a clean bag.

Clean the connections using isopropyl alcohol and/or lint-free swabs.

Remove dust particles with a pressured optical duster before installation, during mating, and after cleaning.

Ensure that metal keys will fit within the container - never over-tighten optical connectors.

FIBER JUMPERS / PATCH CORDS

The optical signal from the transmitter is carried by two different types of optical transmission medium equipment. Fiber cables, patch cords, and fiber jumpers are among them.

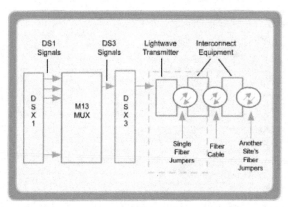

The transmitter outputs the optical light wave signal via fiber jumpers or patch cables.

An optical transmission medium may be found in the jumpers. Super pure glass fiber serves as the medium, offering a low-loss channel for the transmission of light wave signals.

The light wave transmitter is cross-connected to the light wave connecting equipment via fiber jumpers.

The Network Element (or NE) or Interconnecting Fiber Distribution Frames are the usual jumpers from the Fiber Distribution Frame.

FIBER OPTIC CABLES

Copper and fiber optic cables are both used in the outside plant. Depending on the manufacturer, the extremely pure glass cable arrangement may hold up to 864 fiber cables or more.

Another form of fiber cable utilized within the CO is a tie cable, which connects two fiber distribution frames.

The fiber is terminated at the interconnect equipment at remote terminal locations, and it is cross-connected to the light wave equipment via fiber jumpers. The fiber optic hardware functions the same way it does at the central office.

Interconnections

Interconnection in telecommunications is the act of physically connecting a carrier's network to hardware or infrastructure that is not a part of that network.

The phrase can refer to a connection between two (or more) carriers or a link between a carrier's infrastructure and its customer's equipment.

Next, let's examine the connecting hardware.

INTERCONNECTION EQUIPMENT

The fiber optic network's interconnect equipment enables the connecting of fiber lines. It offers a way to terminate OSP plant fiber cables that are entering the Remote Terminal, Hub, or Central Office, to be more precise.

The OSP cables and equipment are interfaced via the interconnecting equipment. For OSP fibers, it offers a central access point for testing. It enables quick fiber channel rearrangements and the coupling of lightwave transmission systems.

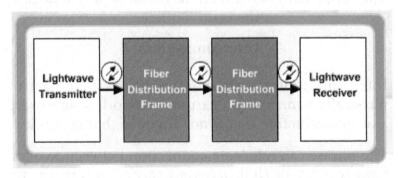

Let's look at the components of the fiber distribution frame:

The Fiber Distribution Frame (FDF), which supports the interconnection requirements for customers, couriers, and other telecommunications providers, switches, transport equipment, and cable facilities in a specific CO or wire center, is regarded as a crucial component of the Central Office or Hut Remote Terminal.

The OSP terminated fiber is cross-linked to the CO terminating equipment at the FDF.

The FDF can also be put on the customer's premises or at a remote terminal as it serves as a cross-connect point between OSP and distribution (F2) facilities or customer cabling in this location. Optical jumpers with connections at both ends are used to create the cross-connect.

STANDARD FIBER DISTRIBUTION FRAME

The medium density FDF is the standard FDF for the largest local exchange companys. The size is 23" wide on the inside, 26" wide on the outside, and 15" deep. It has up to 9 panels per 7' high bay, or up to 648 FOTs, and has 72 fiber ports per panel. Office or OSP Hut Remote Terminals are used in places with light to medium traffic volumes.

A high-density FDF that has a different frame structure comprises a multi-trough HD bay configuration with a high-density 72 port panel. It won't fit in a frame relay rack that is standard. It must fit in a big bay layout that is 36" wide and 36" deep, even though its real dimensions are 26" wide and 40" deep. Up to 1440 FOTs may be installed in each bay of this FDF. It would be utilized in areas with moderate to high traffic.

Fiber Distribution Frame

A centralized location for managing and organizing the fiber optic facility is offered by the FDF. It offers a flexible foundation for future fiber expansion and offers connections that may be rearranged between two connections or appearances.

The FDF components are **Connector Panel** – where terminations are made, **Splicing Tray,** and the **Fiber Management Storage Trays (FMT)** that hold excess fiber optic jumper cables.

CENTRAL OFFICE EQUIPMENT – FIBER TRANSPORT

Additional CO equipment for digital transmission over fiber may consist of the following devices:

Fiber Multiplexer (Mux):

For transit via fiber infrastructure, multiplex one or more DS3s and convert an electrical signal into an optical signal. Demultiplex the digital signal after converting the received OC3 from an optical signal to an electrical signal.

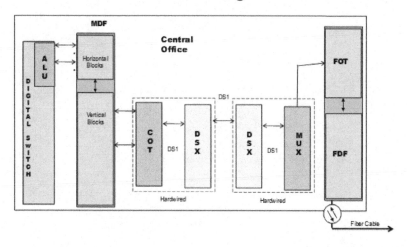

Fiber Distribution Frame (FDF):

Can be indicated as a Fiber Optical Termination panel (FOT) or an LGX, depending on regional preferences. Like DSX panels used for cross-connecting copper cables, FDFs are Interconnection points for fiber optic transmission equipment.

CONNECTOR MODULE USAGE

There are terminations at the front and back of the frame in the connection module.

In the front are jumpers that link to the Fiber Optic Terminations (FOT) machinery and jumpers that connect to the terminated OSP directly. Additionally, the OSP cable termination patch wires are in front of the frame.

Fibers from the equipment to the FOT and OSP cables to the vault are linked at the back of the frame.

Connector module components:

Connector Plates provide a mounting point for bulkhead adapters. It holds up to 96 adapters depending on the chosen option. They are divided into two groups, one on left and one on right. Each group has mounting space for up to 48 adapters on each side

Designation Cards, front and rear, are used to label cable to equipment connectivity.

Patch Cord Fanning Strips on either side of the plate help maintain an acceptable bend radius when routing cords in the vertical channel

Front Cover prevents the patch cord connector from being disturbed by normal frame activity.

Splice Module

When splicing pigtails to optical fibers, a safe enclosure is provided by the splice module to place splice trays and coil up the service loop. The chassis, splice drawers, sleeve kit, and cover make up the splice module.

Splice drawers may be simply taken out and mounted on a track.

Each splice drawer may accommodate two splice trays. Each drawer has metal tabs and different cable retainers for coiling up service loops.

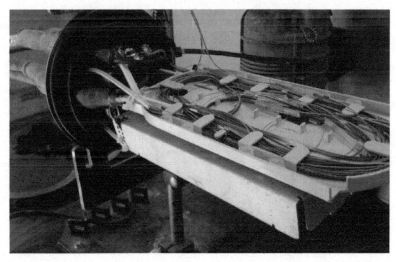

The sleeve kit stops the pigtails from binding within each splice drawer. Pigtails are braided into groups of 12 and wrapped in sleeves of fiberglass to provide protection.

Fusion, heat-shrink, mechanical, or rotary fiber lock splice trays can all be used with the splice module. Each splice module may accommodate up to 16 splice trays.

Storage Module

Patch cables are kept in the storage module. In the front of the frame, the Cable Management Trays (CMTs) offer a practical location for storing extra patch cord length. A CMT may support up to 36 different patch cables separately. Each tray can hold two individual patch cables and has a storage capacity of 26 feet.

All patch cables that are kept in storage retain a minimum bend radius of 2".

Cable and equipment can be terminated in the same enclosure in small office applications. Fiber optic equipment is located in the front, while OSP cable is terminated at the back.

Elements

For fiber optic termination, there are several cable routing strategies. A single fiber distribution frame bay in an office with many bays is shown in the diagram above.

OSP cables will typically end at the connection module at the base of the bay. To make CO fiber optic terminations, patch cables are routed to the top of the bay. The CMT, which is directly above the CO connection module, is where extra patch cord lengths are kept.

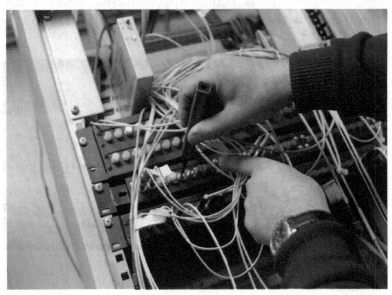

SUMMARY

An overview of fiber optic history, theory, and applications was covered in this guide. The main topics covered are the development of fiber optic communications equipment, the distinction between copper wire and fiber optics, and the fundamentals of fiber technology and its application in today's passive optical network technology.

Books currently in progress, or already published in this series, are:

Outside Plant Engineer Job Descriptions

Conventional Cable Transmission for the OSPE I

Taking Field Notes for the OSPE I

Bonding and Grounding for the OSPE I

Aerial Plant and Guying for the OSPE II

FTTX Planning and Design for the OSPE II

Project Management for the OSPE III

OUTSIDE PLANT
ENGINEERING 101

Books in planning stages at this time are:

Underground Plant and conduit for the OSPE II

Direct Buried Plant for the OSPE II

OSPE Acronyms for the OSPE I

REFERENCES:

John Bairds's Facimile Machine
Soundandcommunications.com

Alexander Graham Bell's Photophone
Thoughtco.com

Practices and Specifications
AT&T Clr's

Practices and Specifications
Sprint Telecom

Paid Stock images
Dreamstime, Inc

Made in the USA
Coppell, TX
03 December 2024

41675366R00046